Being Successful in

G000146798

About the Author

Harris Rosenberg BA(Hons), DMS, MCIM, MIMng is acknowledged as the UK's leading expert on business and other grants. His experience has been built up over many years, both in business and in the fields of corporate funding, sourcing finance and grant application. He is a member of the Institute of Management, the Chartered Institute of Marketing and an Expert Witness. He is the author of five books, including two publications for the DTI, and a contributor to many publications relating to various aspects of grants, financing and business development. As the leading consultant in this complex field, he is a regular contributor to television and radio presentations and frequently delivers lectures and seminars to banks, companies, agencies and institutes.

How to apply for Grants, Loans and other Sources of Finance (Gee Publishing Ltd, 1993, 1994, 1995, 1998).

Russia: Market Approaches – The Different Business Digest (DTI/FCO – Gee Publishing Ltd, 1994, 1997) – co-written with David Cant.

How to reduce your Commercial Rates and Utility Costs (Gee Publishing Ltd, 1996) – co-written with Jonathan Wolf.

One Stop Finance (Prentice Hall, ICSA, 1997).

A Handbook of School Fundraising (Kogan Page, 1998).

Sector Report: British Fashion in Russia – Opportunities for British Companies (DTI, 1996).

Being Successful in . . .
Report Writing

Harris Rosenberg

BLACKHALL
Publishing

This book was typeset by
Gough Typesetting Services for
BLACKHALL PUBLISHING
· 26 Eustace Street
Dublin 2
Ireland

e-mail: blackhall@tinet.ie

ISBN: 1 901657 19 1

A catalogue record for this book is available from the
British Library.

Printed in Ireland by
Betaprint Ltd

Series Foreword

*The Being Successful in...*series is a new series of practical books, which provides an accessible and user friendly approach to the common problems experienced by small to medium-sized, growing businesses.

The series will help businesses in the start-up phase but also covers problems encountered during the all-important development phase. They will be helpful to businesses which are starting to grow, and which need to cope with a range of unfamiliar, difficult and often competing issues.

The books in the series are comprehensive and yet concise, and they treat the topics in question succinctly and without recourse to jargon. Practical examples, checklists and pointers on to further sources of help and advice are included to supplement the text.

Books published in early 1999:
Being Successful in...Report Writing
Being Successful in...Customer Care
Being Successful in...Motivation
Being Successful in...Trademarks & Patents
Being Successful in...Time Management
Being Successful in...Budgeting

Forthcoming books in the series:

Being Successful in...Presentations
Being Successful in...Managing Your Business
                              Performance
Being Successful in...Managing Your People
                              Performance
Being Successful in...Overcoming Stress
Being Successful in...Winning Business
Being Successful in...Business Planning
Being Successful in...Public Relations

I hope you find this book useful.

Veronica Canning
December 1998

Contents

Dedication

To my parents, Hilda and Jack Rosenberg.

Acknowledgements

I would like to thank the following for their help and advice.

- ❖ Gregg Berlie – Blue Mountain Community College
- ❖ Sue Carter
- ❖ Joseph Faith
- ❖ Ann Henderson – Pre-school Learning Alliance
- ❖ Erica Payne
- ❖ Aaron Rosenberg
- ❖ Michelle Rosenberg
- ❖ Philip Rosenberg
- ❖ Samantha Rosenberg

Introduction

One day, a colleague stated, "I do not know how to write a report." I replied, "You just did." Every day all of us make reports. A report is the summation of the written or spoken word. It may state historic information, a present state of being or predict future events based upon given information.

The aim of this book will be to remove the fear or concern that confronts the person needing to prepare a report. This book will guide you on how to prepare a written or oral report, encourage you to use best practice and avoid the pitfalls that may weaken your chances of success.

This publication will assist you to prepare a report or presentation for a board meeting, line manager, interviewing committee or any other body or individual that you need to impress. Above all, it will teach you how to be successful in making your report.

I hope this report on the book has been helpful.

Harris Rosenberg
December 1998

Chapter 1

What Is A Report?

This chapter will define:

- what a report is for;
- who a report is for;
- why a report is wanted;
- how a report should be presented.

It will also tell you:

- what to avoid in preparing the report.

What Is A Report?

Standard dictionaries define the word 'report' in a number of ways. Principally, they describe a report as a written or oral statement describing or narrating one or more events that have passed. In this definition, a report provides an account of information received and interpreted by the author or narrator.

A report is a tool of analysis prepared by one or more people for others. The word 'report' is also used to describe a written or oral discussion of the results of an investigation, a statement of progress or a declaration of predicted outcomes. As a result of this, a reader or listener will be able to make an informed decision about, for example, whether or not to lend money to a business.

Another definition of the word 'report' is in its use as a noun. A school report, for example, is a communication by a school, to a pupil's parents, relating to the progress of the child. A *Which? Report* will describe the merits or otherwise of goods and services. It could also be descriptive, e.g. a man of good report. Lastly, the word 'report' can be used as a verb, e.g. to report fit.

Reports may be routine, e.g. monthly sales reports, or non-routine, e.g. a report leading to a capital purchase.

In all cases, the word 'report' tells the reader or listener something. It passes on information.

This idea is powerfully expressed by the Australian Economic Co-operation Programme. It states that the main purpose of a report is:

> *. . . to inform, advise, persuade, precede or up-date, interpret, confront problems, answer questions, suggest options [and] to communicate information. . .*

In addition:

> *. . . it answers the questions of who, what, where, when, why and how. It is logical and accurate. It is concise yet complete. It identifies all areas of regulatory concern . . . clearly, succinctly, factually and objectively.*
>
> Environmental Protection Agency
> USA

The style, form and content of a report can vary immensely, but to be successful in making your report the following ingredients are vital.

WHO REQUIRES THE REPORT?

Knowing to whom a report is to be presented should be the critical factor in determining:
- the purpose of the report;
- the style of the report;
- the length of the report.

Purpose

The United States Environmental Protection Agency describes a report as being a "permanent product of an inspection or investigation". This, it continues, is unlikely to be physically presented by you. You must know why the report has been commissioned or requested. Always remember any terms of reference. The purpose of the report could be:

- *to describe a present situation*, this would enable the recipient to make decisions based upon factual evidence, e.g. a stock report;
- *to determine why a situation has occurred and make recommendations for change*, e.g. an inquiry into an accident or crime;
- *to provide comparative information*, this will encourage change or improvement, using other organisations as exemplars, e.g. school league tables.

The Information Need

The purpose of the report will often determine the content and size of the item presented. Different levels of information need must be considered. These will be determined by the reader or audience.

WORD TO THE WISE

All reports should address the interest of the reader or audience.

Appropriate for the Reader

Knowing your audience is critical. All reports should address the interest of the reader or audience. A report aimed at young children would be very different to one prepared for adults. Account would need to be taken of the information to be imparted, the language used and any instructions to be followed by the recipient. Use of pictures and diagrams may help with this.

Account must also be taken of the level of expertise of the reader or audience, a report written for a layman would be very different to that written for an expert. The layman, by the nature of his lack of knowledge, would not be familiar with the subject matter or the terminology used in a certain discipline.

Knowledge of the reader's ability and authority to act upon a report should also be considered. If the reader is not able to act directly upon recommendations, it is important to know who they must persuade. For example, a sales report outlining the benefits of a machine may be excellent technically but fail to obtain a sale if it does not prove the machine provides value for money.

Timing

Reports are always written for a purpose. This will often dictate the time allowed for the work. An academic report or dissertation will have to be delivered by a specific date in a given term; a business report for a given meeting; a newspaper report for the same evening. Failure to meet deadlines may be critical making any work undertaken, and delivered late, worthless.

Style

The style of a report will vary according to whom it is for. The chart below indicates the form the report may take.

STYLE OF REPORT

Formal	Informal
Written	Oral
Letter	Memo
Narrative	Graphic
Prose	Numeric
Analytical	Speculative
Investigative	Suggestive
Individual	Group
Provocative	Conciliatory
Descriptive	Proactive
Detailed	Summary

Length

A report is meant to convey information quickly and easily. Even long reports should be able to do this through an abstract and concluding summary. Where a report is investigative, it is good practice to include the following:

- contents list;
- abstract of the report;
- conclusion and recommendations.

The abstract, conclusion and recommendations will summarise the nature and findings of a report. Should further information be required, the reader could refer to the contents list to find sections of specific interest.

Occasionally, the length of a report is determined by the person wishing to receive it. The reader may wish to form his own conclusions and therefore ask for evidence allowing him to do so. In such cases, it is usual for the reviewer to have an application form. Examples of application forms seeking specific information include government grant applications.

In many instances, application forms will not be given but standard information will nevertheless be required. Business plans and curriculum vitae are examples of these.

INFORMATION OVERKILL

A report needs to impart information. Nonetheless, it must always be remembered that time is needed by a readership or audience to assimilate this information. Discipline is needed in discriminating information into that which is important and that which is of subsidiary benefit. This is not easy. Knowledge, experience and subjectivity will all colour the judgement of the author.

PRESENTING THE INFORMATION IN THE MANNER REQUIRED

The style of a report may be pre-determined by the organisation for which it is being written. Some organisations have 'house styles'. Guidelines on this will be given before any report is commissioned. (See Chapter 5: Layout And Design.)

REMEMBER

DO

- Remember who the report is for.

- Remember why they wanted it.

- Remember how they wanted it presented.

- Write an abstract for longer reports.

- Use diagrams if appropriate.

- Use any 'house style'.

DO NOT

- Overestimate the reader's knowledge.

- Use unfamiliar words (jargon).

- Write more than is required.

- Be subjective.

Chapter 2

What Form Should A Report Take?

This chapter will help you to:

• determine the type of report to be written.

It will also teach you:

• how to devise a contents list;

• what should be included in each section;

• the emphasis to be placed on each section of the report.

What Form Should A Report Take?

The form a report should take will depend upon who it is for. Three types of report may be required:

- short, factual;
- standard response;
- investigative.

SHORT, FACTUAL REPORTS

A short, factual report will be a presentation of information required for immediate information purposes. Examples include a company's balance sheet, a cashflow, stock report, list of employees or curriculum vitae.

All these reports should be short – ideally one page or less – following a set, and therefore predictable, format.

STANDARD RESPONSE REPORTS

These reports should be written to the style and in the format required by the reader. Do not give additional information unless it is specifically requested or you have permission to do so.

Example

Please give a brief history of the applicant business (e.g. when formed and any recent major developments), trends in trading performance and reasons for any significant variations in sales and gross/net margins.

(If you need more space, please use a separate sheet of paper.)

The above example has been taken from an application form for Regional Selective Assistance, a grant offered by the UK Department of Trade and Industry to businesses in specified areas.

INVESTIGATIVE REPORTS

Investigative reports are discussed in more detail below and may take a number of forms including:

- empirical research reports;
- hypotheses;
- feasibility studies;
- proposals.

Empirical Research Reports

Empirical research reports analyse a problem based on existing knowledge and research as well as first-hand research, report all relevant data and can include solutions to the problem or problems. An empirical research report then concludes whether solutions are workable.

Gregg Berlie
Blue Mountain Community College
Oregon

Such research reports are based on careful and detailed investigation, original research and study. These may be undertaken in a laboratory or in the field, through interviews or research undertaken in a library. Empirical reports are written to share knowledge discovered and usually include a review of published literature on the subject. Empirical research reports will usually follow the following format.

1. Title.
2. Abstract.
3. Introduction and review of previous research literature.
4. Materials and methods of research.
5. Results.
6. Discussion of the significance of the results.
7. Conclusion.
8. References (works cited or bibliography).
9. Appendices of all relevant data.

Hypotheses

Unlike empirical research reports, hypotheses are based upon intelligent guesswork. When examining a hypothesis, research methodology is used to test whether your assumption is correct. A report on a hypothesis will usually follow the following format.

1. Title.
2. Abstract.
3. Background information leading to the assumption.
4. Materials and methods of research.

5. Results.
6. Discussion of the significance of the results.
7. Conclusion.
8. References.
9. Appendices of all relevant data.

Feasibility Studies

Feasibility studies analyse the situation to determine the possible solutions to questions surrounding the problem or situation and indicate the best solution in comparison to alternative solutions. The organisation includes a comparison and contrast format . . . Feasibility studies look at options, ideas or products to see if they can be implemented and to see which one is preferable. A number of issues must be considered including cost and practicality.

Gregg Berlie
Blue Mountain Community College
Oregon

Unlike an empirical research report, feasibility studies will emphasise particular findings or advance one solution. Feasibility studies will follow the following format.

1. Title.
2. Abstract.
3. Introduction.
4. Materials and methods of research.
5. Results.
6. Comparison of possible solutions, weighing strengths and weaknesses of each.

7. Conclusion.
8. Recommendations.
9. References.
10. Appendices of relevant data.

Proposals

> *Proposals analyse a specific problem, recommending a solution to this. It will state all relevant data and recommend the person or management who are to implement the solution. Proposals are often written in response to request for consultancy advice.*
>
> Gregg Berlie
> Blue Mountain Community College
> Oregon

Initially, the proposal will emanate from:

• a request for a proposal;

• a request for a quotation;

• a statement of work to be undertaken;

• an unsolicited offer of help.

The nature of the amount of work required for each of the above forms of proposal will vary. Requests for proposals will require significantly more work, including analysis of information, than the unsolicited proposal which may require little more than the introductory information. Proposals will follow the following format.

1. Proposal description.

    (a) Introduction with a statement of the problem.

    (b) Rationale significance.

    (c) Facilities and equipment.

2. Schedule of implementation.

3. Personnel who will implement the proposal.

4. Budget.

5. Evaluation system to measure effectiveness.

6. Expected benefits.

Proposals will state recommendations in their introduction.

FORMAT OF INVESTIGATIVE REPORTS

An investigative report will contain four main sections. Although the length may not be determinable, the writer should always remember that quality not quantity is critical. The four main sections of the report comprise:

• introduction;

• main body;

• conclusions;

• recommendations.

Introduction

This should be no more than 15 per cent of the report total. It should comprise the following elements.

Always

- Preliminary information.
- Scope of the report.
- Purpose and background to the report.
- Aims of the report.

Optional

- Problems resolved or questions to be asked.
- Procedure.
- Methodology including how the report is structured.

The introduction should be clear and unambiguous. It should include a brief summary of findings and indicate any restrictions or lack of information that may be relevant.

Main Body

> **WORD TO THE WISE**
>
> The main body should comprise about 80 per cent of the report.

This should comprise about 80 per cent of the report. This will present the main information of the report and results of all investigations. It will provide an analysis and interpretation on the data described. It should contain clear sections, with each section being linked together in a logical format. Opinions of others should be stated as opinions, not as facts.

In scientific, technical or mathematical reports, detailed workings and calculations will be found in this section.

Conclusion

This should comprise no more than 15 per cent of the report. It should always refer to the report's purpose. It may be proactive or neutral. The former style will summarise the main findings of the report and give clear recommendations to the reader. It will contain no new information. The latter form, which is less common, will present facts in an unbiased and logical manner, allowing the reader to form his own opinion based upon evidence presented.

Recommendations

Where a number of recommendations are to be made, it may be clearer to write them as a separate section. This section may include a recommendation for further investigations, if necessary. It is often helpful to list any recommendations in numerical order.

REMEMBER

DO

- Answer the question(s) asked.
- Present your report in the style requested.
- Remember the importance of an abstract.
- Remember the function of the concluding section.
- Remember that the body of the report should contain detailed information.
- Be relevant.

DO NOT

- Waffle.
- Guess information – research it.

Chapter 3

Style Of The Report

This chapter will:

- remind you why you are writing the report;
- help you plan each section of your report;
- help you write each section of your report;
- give you tips on the appropriate style for each type of report that may be required;
- help you to prepare a bibliography.

Style Of The Report

Reports may follow various formats, the most common being:

- the information sheet;
- the instruction sheet;
- the short report;
- the long report;
- the interactive report.

THE INFORMATION SHEET

The information sheet or fact sheet is a report of one page. It contains relevant facts required by the reader in a succinct form, allowing decisions to be made or instructions to be followed with ease. It must leave no room for mis- interpretation.

Whilst the structure of an information sheet will vary according to the purpose, it will often comprise the following components.

- Administrative details, e.g. file references, readership, date of issue, date of period covered.
- Title.
- Points of attention.

Style Of The Report

Reports may follow various formats, the most common being:

- the information sheet;
- the instruction sheet;
- the short report;
- the long report;
- the interactive report.

THE INFORMATION SHEET

The information sheet or fact sheet is a report of one page. It contains relevant facts required by the reader in a succinct form, allowing decisions to be made or instructions to be followed with ease. It must leave no room for mis- interpretation.

Whilst the structure of an information sheet will vary according to the purpose, it will often comprise the following components.

- Administrative details, e.g. file references, readership, date of issue, date of period covered.
- Title.
- Points of attention.

Administrative Details

Administrative details may be appropriate, on an information sheet, for several purposes.

- To identify and to specify the readership.

- To allow for storage or retrieval.

- To indicate relevance of information.

The necessity of any of the above details will depend upon the bespoke requirements of the report and the readership. Being a method of communication, it is useful to indicate to whom the information is given, or not given if the nature of the organisation is confidential, e.g. a job application. A readership list will allow the readership to communicate with each other on the understanding that all have equal knowledge.

Although information sheets may be useful for records, they can, like any other source of data, be retained beyond their useful life and therefore accumulate unnecessarily. Housekeeping is vital. It is, therefore, useful to date information sheets. This will tell the reader whether the information is current.

Title

An information sheet should always have a title. It should be short, bold and self-explanatory, for example, 'Stock Record'.

The title, at a glance, will tell the reader what the report is and give an indication of its importance.

Points of Attention

The purpose of an information sheet is to provide information allowing the reader to either:

- make a decision;
- provide instruction to undertake a particular task.

> The form the information takes will depend upon its purpose. It could be:
>
> - numeric;
> - graphic, e.g. a graph, pie chart or bar chart;
> - diagrammatic, e.g. a pie chart;
> - descriptive.

Where the written word is used, the sentences should be short. In all instances, the information sheet will need to give information in an easily digestible form.

THE INSTRUCTION SHEET

Like an instruction sheet, an information sheet outlines:

- processes that must be meticulously followed;
- the method by which those processes must be undertaken;
- an indication of a result that will be achieved.

Often instruction sheets will use graphics. Unlike an information sheet, instructions may be given on one or more pages.

> **Examples of instruction sheets include:**
>
> - do-it-yourself assembly units;
> - model-making kits;
> - fire and emergency instructions;

- safety instructions;
- warning notices.

Instruction sheets should be written in the imperative. For example:

- Do not open the door.
- In case of fire, break glass.

THE SHORT REPORT

Short reports are similar to information sheets or fact sheets. By definition they are short and also have one of two functions:

- to present facts;
- to present facts and the reporter's interpretation of them.

Factual Reports

The short, factual report will address the following.

How	The report of an incident.
What	A list of items required.
When	Dates of meetings.
Where	Flight programme information.
Who	Statements by an individual.

Interpretative Reports

In addition to facts, an interpretative report will give the view of the author. It may, for example, include information on why a certain situation prevails and offer an evaluation of it. It should also include recommendations for future action.

The components of a short report will include:

*   administrative details;
*   title;
*   terms of reference;
*   introduction;
*   main body of the report;
*   conclusions and recommendations;
*   appendices.

Administrative Details

Administrative details are appropriate in a report, for several reasons:

*   to identify and specify the readership;
*   to allow for storage or retrieval;
*   to indicate relevance of information.

The necessity of any of the above details will depend upon the bespoke requirements of the report and the readership. Being a method of communication, it is useful to indicate to whom the information is given, or not given if the nature of the organisation is confidential, e.g. a job application. A readership list will allow the readership to communicate with each other on the understanding that all have equal knowledge.

Although information sheets may be useful for records, they can, like any other source of data, be retained beyond their useful life and therefore accumulate unnecessarily. Housekeeping is vital. It is, therefore, useful to date reports. This will tell the reader whether the information is current.

Title

A report should always have a title. It should be short, bold and self-explanatory, for example, 'Monthly Sales Report'.

The title, at a glance, will tell the reader what the report is and give an indication of its importance.

Terms of Reference

Terms of reference may not always be required. This will depend upon:

- at whom the information is aimed;
- who gave the instruction for the report to be devised.

The terms of reference will outline the reasons why the report is needed. These may take one of two forms:

- Result of an instruction, e.g. "This report has been commissioned to examine . . . "
- Functional, e.g. "Progress report on. . . " or "Status report on . . . "

The terms of reference may also give an introduction to the report outlining:

- for whom it is intended;
- factual background.

Introduction

An introduction, unlike terms of reference, will start the report with factual information, including the reasons for writing the report.

Main Body

The main body of the report will provide the information required by the reader. Unlike information sheets, a short report will be required to provide analysis and interpretation of the data.

Conclusions and Recommendations

This section will provide, in brief detail, recommendations and steps to be followed. It should not outline the reasons for the suggestions made. These should appear in the main body of the report.

Appendices

The appendices will provide all, or some of, the following information, as required:

* glossary of terms;

* contact information;

* sources of information;

* evidence;

* bibliography.

Housekeeping

A short report is usually not required to show evidence or provide information sources. It is, however, prudent to retain such information in an accessible form. It is not unknown for readers to require evidence justifying the conclusions reached by the report writer.

THE LONG REPORT

A long report is a piece of work that has been thoroughly researched, where the data collected has been verified and interpreted and then tested for accuracy and objectivity.

It is not meant to prompt its reader to immediate action, its aim is to be thought provoking. Just as time and detail will have been taken to comprise the report, the reactions to it should be measured.

A long report, whilst reaching conclusions, should always give options by stating the assessed consequences of inaction or inertia. It may be defined not just by its length, which by implication would be more than four, A4 pages, but by the detail that it contains.

The components of a long report will include:

- covering sheet;
- title page;
- front page;
- contents section;
- terms of reference;
- abstract;
- introduction;
- main body;
- conclusions;
- recommendations;
- annexes;
- appendices;
- bibliography.

Covering Sheet

The covering sheet will be a letterhead. It will state the nature of the enclosure. The letterhead will provide:

- a reference for filing;
- the date upon which the report is circulated or made public;
- contact details for further information.

Title Page

The title should state the nature of the report. Where a short title does not convey the full nature of the text, a sub-title should also be given. This page will not be numbered.

The title page must show:

- **Who wrote the report.** The author may be an individual or a group of people, e.g. a parliamentary report, which would be written usually by a committee under the chairmanship of an appointee.

- **The date of the report.**

- **The name of the commissioning body**. This may also be included. The organisation or academic body for whom the report is being written. This information, however, is more likely to be on the front page.

Front Page

The report should state clearly at whom the information is aimed and whether or not the information contained is to be in the public domain. Security information, including copyright details, must be prominently displayed.

Contents Section

The reasons for including a contents page are to:

- provide the reader with easy access, through page numbering, to sections of greatest interest;

- indicate the flow of the report;

- describe the information contained in the report.

In a long report, the contents list may include headings as well as sub-headings of each section. The contents page should not contain greater divisions than sub-headings. Further subdivision would lead to a lack of clarity.

The contents section may include more than the list of contents. It could include:

- a list of tables;

- a list of figures or illustrations;

- an introduction;

- acknowledgements;

- a glossary.

Where acknowledgements are given, they should be relevant and business-like. The name followed by the organisation of a contributor should be mentioned. Where substantial help has been given, you may wish to include an introductory paragraph to give particular thanks to those individuals. Be selective in this.

Terms of Reference

The terms of reference will state the parameters of the study.

Abstract or Executive Summary

An abstract is a summary of the report. It should be between 200 and 400 words, i.e. not more than one, A4 page in length when typed single space. Its aim is to help the reader get a quick grasp of what the report is about, its key features and an indication of conclusions drawn and recommendations arising therefrom.

Although the abstract will be at the beginning of the report, it is normally one of the last items to be written.

Introduction

The introduction should set out:

• relevant background information;

• reasons for the report, including a brief evaluation of present thoughts on your chosen subject;

• an indication of the areas covered.

It may also contain a preface stating permissions obtained to use text or diagrams, which are in copyright, and acknowledgements thanking those who have helped with the report.

Main Body

This section should consist of:

• the facts;

• statements from sources researched.

The author should avoid going beyond the terms of reference. Drawing analogies from other disciplines or sources, providing they are relevant, is acceptable, e.g. a report outlining crowd safety at football matches in the UK could make reference to other sports or other football grounds in the rest of the world.

> **WORD TO THE WISE**
>
> The main body of the report should comprise an analysis of all evidence used. It should be presented in an organised, coherent, logical and usable form.

The main body of the report should not contain the opinions of the author. It should comprise an analysis of all evidence used and should be presented in an organised, coherent, logical and usable form.

It should also mention any difficulties encountered when trying to obtain information. An example of this would be a report on procurement methods of the Ministry of Defence. This may not contain information on a specific type of procurement owing to its classified nature.

Once the report has been compiled, it should be checked for inaccuracies, irrelevancies, anomalies, contradictions and gaps. It is good practice to check information with an original source, contributor or interviewee to ensure that there has been no misinterpretation of information used. When completed, check again the text for spelling mistakes, grammatical errors and readability. Where annexes and appendices are used, they should be referred to in the appropriate sections of the text.

Conclusions

The conclusions section will sum up the findings of the report. It must be short, sharp and relevant. The conclusion will evaluate facts discussed in the text. It will not include the writer's personal opinion.

> **WORD TO THE WISE**
>
> Conclusions must be short, sharp and relevant.

Recommendations

Recommendations may not always be required in a report. If they are, they will state the actions that the author suggests should be taken in light of the evidence produced, which may include future work on the project. Recommendations made should arise logically from the text, be sequential and stated. They should also be itemised. Recommendations may state not only the problem or problems to be solved, but also realistic and achievable solutions to them.

Annexes

Annexes are sections of the report that comprise large amounts of text and data. This section may reproduce evidence or text or other material prepared by the author. Annexes are to be avoided where the information can be readily placed in an appropriate section within the report, as annexes are usually long examples, which would disrupt the flow of the main body of the text if included therein. It may also include charts, maps, tables and diagrams. Annexes may also include text that is referred to in several sections of the report, e.g. a report on the US Bill of Rights may give the full text of this legislation in an annex.

Appendices

Similar to annexes, appendices are data or information, which is essential to a report, and should be included within the main body. Appendices will usually include lists of information, e.g. address lists or long lists of examples which may, if placed in the main body, hinder the reader's understanding of the material.

Appendices should be numbered, unless there is only one. Their order should follow the sequence by which they were first referred to in the main body of the report.

Bibliography

A bibliography section will include all written material to whch reference has been made in the report. A bibliography may be divided into subsections to indicate references from books, newspapers and magazines, internet sources, etc.

THE INTERACTIVE REPORT

An interactive report, by definition, is one that is compiled by more than one person. Those involved in report writing will see the impact of the changes they make immediately. Interactive reports are written generally on computer networks, which may include the internet.

Procedures should also be developed whereby any changes can be easily identified, verified and accepted by other contributors. When interactive reports are being written, it is prudent to have back-up procedures to prevent corruption. Information supplied by contributors should always be checked thoroughly.

BIBLIOGRAPHIES

A bibliography is usually found at the end of a report or sections within a report and indicates sources of information. Sources within a bibliography should be listed alphabetically, ususally by author. Where information obtained is from a variety of sources, the writer may wish to divide the bibliography into sections.

Examples of Material that can be included in a Bibliography

- Books.
- Newspapers, magazines and periodicals.
- Leaflets and brochures.
- Internet sources.

Bibliographical data may include any, or all, of the following elements.

- Name of the author. The surname should precede the christian names and any initials.

- Complete title of the source. Where a chapter from a compilation is used, this should be referred to specifically.

- Name of publisher.

- ISBN number.

- Date of publication.

- Edition number.

- Full internet address and date of retrieval.

- Date of newspaper or magazine. Reference should be made to the headline article and author, if known.

REMEMBER

DO

- Remember at whom the report is aimed.
- Remember the purpose of the report.
- Remember the report's terms of reference.
- Remember the form the report should take.
- Remember the purpose of each section of the report.
- Remember to be relevant.

DO NOT

- Forget to give the report a title.
- Forget to state the date of the report.
- Forget to state who wrote the report.
- Forget to give references for retrieval.

Chapter 4

Research, Evaluation And Control Of Information

This chapter will tell you:

- how to undertake research;
- where to find existing information;
- how to obtain new information;
- how to evaluate the information obtained;
- how to sort the information into a structured report.

Research, Evaluation And Control Of Information

The purpose of research is to gather information, to refine new materials and methods for doing a task and extend the limits of data. Research is the act of asking searching questions, of challenging what is already known.

Gregg Berlie
Blue Mountain Community College
Oregon

COMMENCING RESEARCH

Any professional report will undergo criticism. If it is well researched, it will not be able to be faulted on its factual content. Where information provided is wrong or interpretational, it is open to adverse criticism. Research will involve the following processes:

- identification of sources of information;
- accumulation of data;
- selection of information;
- interpretation of facts based upon evidence.

When undertaking research it is important to use methods appropriate for the report and its readership. You should always bear in mind the nature of the report, the level of information obtainable and the time and budget available for it.

A good report, however, will require more than a mere detailing of facts. It will require:

- an innovative approach to selecting data;

- an identification of material that could be analysed;

- a method for verifying information obtained;

- a novel approach to the subject matter.

Information that does not support your theories should not be ignored unless it is factually incorrect, e.g. wrong dates, places, names, etc. Where the facts are correct, the information should be stated to show that there is evidence supporting an alternative view. The importance of this alternative information can be substantiated or minimised, depending upon your own interpretation. It is important to ensure that you have all relevant information. A document ignored or overlooked can render your report worthless. Do not let personal bias colour your comments.

WHERE TO FIND INFORMATION

Finding information may be relatively easy. Initially, much of the information may be known to you from existing sources available at your local library, place of work or home. Gathering further information may equally, through the use of the internet, be undertaken in the comfort of your home surroundings. It is imperative to verify any information taken from the internet to ensure its accuracy, however sound it may appear on first examination. There are also many specialist libraries, e.g. institute libraries, trade association libraries and libraries within goverment departments. Museums and galleries, as well as public archives, contain sources of information that may be relevant to particular topics. When going to specialist libraries, it is prudent to book an appointment beforehand.

SORTING OUT INFORMATION

Whether research is undertaken before ideas are crystallised or ideas are put to paper before research commences is a matter for personal preference. Two indispensable tools that help with this are:

* a spider map;
* a contents list.

Spider Map

Spider maps are sometimes referred to as spray, scatter or patterned notes. A spider map is a diagram from which ideas emanate from a central theme (the short title). All ideas should be put on the spider map as they come to you. The development of a spider map may go through several stages. Once prepared, the items listed may be sorted into a contents list.

Example

I was invited to the Wolfson Hillel Primary School, Southgate to talk to their Year 3 children about how to write a book. I suggested that a book on mammals would be a good topic and asked each of the 22 children to give me one idea of what should be in a book on this subject.

The diagrams below were developed into a contents list for a book, using a spider chart and developments ensuing from it. Writing a report would follow a similar structure.

Diagram 1: Mammals

1.	Lions
2.	Pets
3.	Rat
4.	Cows
5.	Camels
6.	Eating
7.	Human being
8.	Mouse
9.	Warm blooded
10.	Sleeping habits
11.	Lives
12.	Rhinoceros
13.	Hair
14.	Hare
15.	Canines
16.	Teeth
17.	Factory farming
18.	Bat
19.	Vampire bat
20.	Elephant
21.	Giraffe
22.	Omnivore

Diagram 1 shows the 22 topics mentioned by the pupils. It can be seen that there was interaction between different people's ideas, some suggestions emanating from others, e.g. bat and vampire bat. It also shows the topics that were of interest to that particular group.

Diagram 2: Spider Map

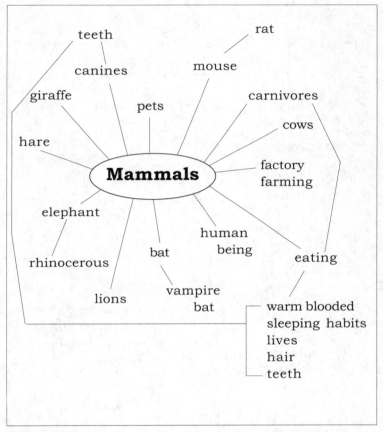

Diagram 2 shows the spider map from the list in Diagram 1. The spider map sorts the topics given in Diagram 1 into an order upon which to base any writing. It is the beginning of a sequencing process. The spider map also shows the interconnection between different ideas, e.g. omnivores and eating, and repeats topics where apt, e.g. teeth.

Diagram 3

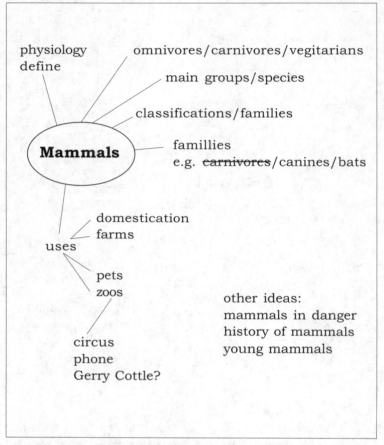

Diagram 3 shows how the spider map evolves through the refining of topics and introduction of new ideas in a regulated order. It also shows how ideas, are being formulated into a contents list. It will be noted that the word carnivores has been crossed out when repeated. Spider maps are not meant to be works of art, they are meant to be practical tools that can be changed and amended to help with the development of your project (where practical make notes of sources of information that come to mind, e.g. telephone Gerry Cottle for in-

formation about circus animals). Reference is also
made to other thoughts that come to mind, e.g.
mammals in danger. It will also be noted that the
word 'vegetarians', rather than 'herbivores', is used.
Errors, due to a lack of knowledge, can always be
corrected throughout the writing process.

Diagram 4: Draft Contents List

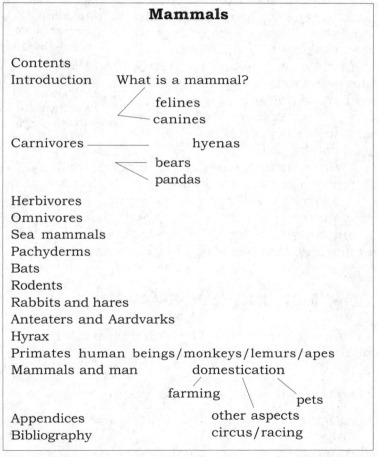

Diagram 4 shows the initial draft contents list.
This has evolved through the interaction of ideas
and moulding of them into a logical format.

CONTENTS

Items to be covered in a contents list have been described in an earlier section (see Chapter 3: The Long Report). It is nevertheless worth reiterating that the contents list is flexible. As writing takes place, some subjects that were thought to be of major importance, may become less so, and others will gain importance. Guidance may also be given by the individual or organisation for which the report is written. As long as the contents remain true to the concept stated, changes will not be criticised.

When writing a report for commercial use, a contents list is often a good method of presenting a proposal. It will outline the structure and subject matter of the report. It will also allow the promoter to recommend amendments and other areas that they wish to have covered.

CONTROLLING INFORMATION

Creating pigeonholes into which information may be placed, will enable you to control the information by:

- accumulating relevant data into one area;
- sifting other information, as it is needed, into appropriate sections

Depending upon the volume and nature of information obtained, it can be separated and stored in:

- ring binders, which separate topics;
- bank boxes;
- sorting trays.

Where the source of information contains several topics, it is often helpful to photocopy the different sections and store them according to your planned writing. Ensure that any photocopies do refer to their original source. It is easy to forget where information came from. If you do photocopy sheets, it is also helpful to make notes on them, showing how, and in which context, the information is to be used.

Serendipity

Often, as one becomes involved in report writing, thoughts will occur at strange times, often in unusual places. It is always helpful to have pen and paper or dictaphone to hand. A flash of inspiration recorded promptly is less likely to be forgotten.

SOURCES OF RESEARCH MATERIAL

Sources of information may vary but basically the premise is always the same: learn as much as you can about a subject. Then see what you can do to learn even more. If others have undertaken research on your topic, start with their findings and build from there. If no one else has done research, become the first to do the research.

Gregg Berlie,
Blue Mountain College
Oregon

GATHERING INFORMATION AND PREPARING THE BIBLIOGRAPHY

There are many sources from which information can be gathered.

- Encyclopaedia, directories, dictionaries, book catalogues, business indexes, newspaper indexes, on-line databanks, CD-ROM data disks, introductory textbooks.

- Books, home pages, newspapers, magazines, journals, research reports, surveys, government documents, parliamentary reports, company brochures, pamphlets, maps, corporate reports, statistics, audio tapes, video tapes, transcripts, sales catalogues, conference and seminar literature and notes, worldwide websites.

- Personal letters, unpublished documents, unpublished films, private records, credit ratings, classified information, internet newsgroups and discussion lists.

Types of Information

Research usually begins with a specific subject, a theory or body of evidence to be outlined and a plan of action. The information that is required will be one of three types:

- tertiary information;

- secondary information;

- primary information.

Tertiary information: This information is of a general nature. It includes information found in encyclopaedia, dictionaries, generalist books including indexes of published articles, general books about a subject and in publications where the relevant information is of secondary or minor importance.

Secondary information: This comprises documents and other materials printed or prepared about the subject in question. This may include written, audio and visual material. These pieces of information provide facts. They also help direct you towards additional research materials, often leading to primary resources.

Primary information: This is first-hand information or primary research. It includes the gathering of unpublished or unresearched facts, performing experiments, collating data and statistics, etc. Primary information may include:

- personal knowledge and experience;
- observation of operations and procedures and of carefully conducted scientific experiments;
- interviews;
- surveys;
- inspection of primary production methods etc.

Sir Isaac Newton stated that his work on gravity was based upon ideas and foundations laid by others – so is the case with all research. A researcher will normally require general information on a subject. This background information is useful, especially if the researcher is unfamiliar with a subject. Secondary information can be considered later, by which time, the researcher will be familiar with terms used and the subject matter of the report. Once fully cognisant with the subject the researcher is able to review critically primary resources and be able to develop his own methods of creating primary data.

One important element of good research is ingenuity. There is more than one way to find information, which may be open or discreet.

Open information: This is readily available to the researcher. It can be accessed from libraries, the internet, archives and other sources.

Discreet information: This is either unpublished or secret. Journalism aims to find discreet information and place it in the public domain.

INTERVIEWS AND QUESTIONNAIRES

An interview is a one-to-one meeting, designed to discover as much relevant information as possible, from an individual in a planned timescale.

A questionnaire is a device to elicit specific information from an individual or group of individuals. The questionnaire may demand written or oral responses from the person being questioned. Whether the questionnaire is to be delivered orally or on paper, it should be tested to iron out ambiguities, misleading questions, questions that do not elicit a clear reply or a required response. Questionnaires may be delivered by post, fax, e-mail or personally through interview (telephone or face to face).

Interviews and questionnaires may be structured, following a logical sequence or semi-structured. Unstructured questionnaires following no logical sequence and eliciting no specific information are not recommended.

Postal Questionnaires

Postal questionnaires, including those administered by fax or e-mail, allow information to be obtained relatively cheaply from a large sample. They also take less time to administer.

Questionnaires may require simple responses, e.g. yes/no answers or preferences. They may also have open-ended questions, eliciting longer answers, e.g. "Please describe why you are seeking this job?"

Avoid double questions, e.g. "Do you think that the South African Rugby Team will win the World Cup and if so why?"

Where questionnaires are given, keep them simple and restrict their length to a maximum of two pages. Longer questionnaires tend to be put aside or not answered at all. Always ensure that questionnaires look pleasing to the eye. Make it easy for respondent to send replies back to you. Enclose an envelope with an address on it. If it can be afforded, use a postage-paid reply service.

Interviews

The Australian Economic Co-operation Programme states that there are four elements to a successful interview:

- the environment;
- the behaviour of the interviewer;
- the information flow;
- the theme.

The interview environment: Interviews should never be interrupted and should be held in private. Never take telephone calls during an interview. Both the interviewer and the interviewee should be comfortable, or as comfortable as possible. Ensure you have space to take notes.

The behaviour of the interviewer: Always try to put your interviewee at ease. Body language is important. Do not try to win arguments. The point of an interview is to obtain information.

The information flow: When interviewing for the purposes of fact finding, ask open-ended questions, e.g. "What do you think of. . . ?" Open-ended questions will alert you to other sources of information. These may also challenge you to devise additional questions leading to a greater knowledge of your subject. Closed questions requiring a 'yes' or 'no' answer do not induce comment or lead to further information being obtained.

It is important to know the interviewee's level of knowledge. Where an in-depth interview is being undertaken, you will be expected to have a certain level of knowledge on the subject, even if it is of a periphery nature. It is prudent to be prepared.

It is professional to give the interviewee advance information of the type of questions you will be asking. When attending the interview dress smartly. If appropriate, wear a business suit.

Always take notes. One or two-word reminders will usually suffice. Do not try to write answers down verbatim. Do not use a tape recorder unless you have specific permission for this, in advance of the interview.

The theme: The purpose of the interview must be kept clearly in mind and you should concentrate and should be organised to obtain required information, as well as new relevant information, in a predefined period of time.

Whilst it is an interviewer's job to make the interviewee feel at ease, the purpose of the interview must not be forgotten. An interview is not a social conversation, although the environment of a social evening may be used to obtain information and to form opinions, it is there to elicit information.

After the interview has taken place, it is prudent to go over any notes and clarify any ambiguitites. It is also good manners to write letters to the interviewees to thank them for their time.

Sampling

For empirical research, the validity of responses to questionnaires, irrespective of the subject matter, will depend upon the sample population tested. Sampling may be random, from a set population/specific audience.

Sampling is not relevant for questionnaires devised for specific purposes, e.g. a questionnaire asking a client about a particular series of events or issues.

Methodology

It is often important to state the control methods used to research information. Where viable alternatives were available, it is important to show why a particular choice was made and another rejected. The methodology used should always be appraised and challenged against information received throughout the report-writing period.

Assumptions and Conclusions

It is acceptable for a report, particularly an investigative report, to make recommendations, providing these are based on facts. The writer should avoid making assumptions. The US Environmental Protection Agency, gives a good example of this.

> *I determined that the records were acceptable after a review of several examples. The most you [may] say is that in your opinion, the specific records reviewed appeared acceptable to you.*

Where comments such as the above are made, it is often helpful to pinpoint the source of the information or availability of data leading to the opinion stated.

REMEMBER

DO

- Research.
- Be ready for inspiration at any time.
- Make notes.
- Evaluate information sources.
- Control information – be systematic.
- State how, and from where, information has been obtained.

DO NOT

- Make assumptions.
- Make questionnaires too difficult to answer.

Chapter 5

Layout And Design

This chapter will teach you:

- the technique required to present a report successfully;

- how to layout your report;

- when and how to use topography;

- when and how to use graphics.

Layout And Design

Layout and design have several objectives:

- to be pleasant to the eye;

- to draw attention to key information, including title and readership;

- to indicate the level of expertise required of the reader.

Whatever the nature of your report, it is important to consider layout and design. Design objectives will always be determined by the nature of your readership. A thesis to be prepared for an academic submission will have its format, style and length stated by the accepting body. Other reports have a style that is determined by usage, for example, an editorial column in a newspaper. Outside these established constraints, the style of layout is a matter of personal choice. Four elements determine the design of a report:

- presentation;

- layout;

- topography;

- graphics.

PRESENTATION

The first visual item a reader will see is the report cover and, where appropriate, a covering letter.

Covering Letters

The style of a covering letter is described in Chapter 3 (The Long Report). If practical, it is recommended that a covering letter should be on good quality paper. The text should all be balanced and pleasing to the eye.

Report Covers

Report covers may vary according to the cost and material available. Lengthy reports should be bound in a rigid or semi-rigid material. The title of a report should be visible through it being:

- printed directly onto the cover;
- neatly pasted on;
- neatly labelled;
- visible through a transparent or translucent cut out or window cut in the front cover. The project title and author's name should be visible through this window.

Reports may be spiral bound, comb bound or heat sealed. Short reports may be bound in acetate folders with a binding rib on the left edge. The acetate and pages should be stapled together, before the plastic rib is slid over, to secure the document. Do not use ring binders.

By convention, British and Irish legal reports are tied together with red tape. Where instructed, you should always follow established procedures. Reports prepared for government grant applications require that information is easily separable. Presenting the information in a bound form, no matter how pleasing to the eye, would cause more work as the report would then need to be subdivided for the several officers who are required to review any application.

LAYOUT

Nothing annoys a reader more than having to flip backwards or forwards while reading your text.

IanStewart
The Business Writing Workbook

Text should be presented attractively. Consistency of form should be sought throughout the text. Formal texts are usually justified to the right of the page. Computer generated or word processed text, by its nature, can be justified to fit the paper used. By convention margins are:

- left margin 1.5";
- right margin 1";
- top margin 1";
- bottom margin 1".

The most common size paper used for reports is A4. Reports should be printed on one side of each piece of paper only. Remember, each page of text is part of a whole.

Cluttering should be avoided. The print quality should be dark and clear. A seriffed font style (e.g. Garamond, *Book Antiqua* or Times Roman or similar) should be used with the point size 12. (This book is printed in Bookman Old Style, point size 11.) Page breaks should occur in sensible places.

> *There is no need to take a new page for each main section heading, but make sure that at least a couple of lines of text follow each heading, otherwise insert a page break before the heading. Never let a page break separate the last line of a paragraph. Try to ensure that, if possible, enumerated lists [(a), (b), (c) etc.] are not split across pages.*
>
> Helen Lowe
> Department of Computer Studies
> Napier University

Reports required for academic usage or text submitted for publication should be typed using double spacing. For some reports bullet points, numbering and lettering are helpful. These will draw a reader's attention to the selected sections.

Use of Paragraphs

It is helpful to write a report using reasonably sized paragraphs. Do not write in short note form. Each paragraph should state a specific point and should lead logically to a following paragraph, developing an argument or listing points in systematic order.

WORD TO THE WISE

It is helpful to write a report using reasonably sized paragraphs.

Try to keep paragraphs to between three and ten sentences. Where a paragraph is long, owing to its content, you may consider use of bullet points or italics to draw a reader's attention to important statements. This will have two effects:

• it will make the paragraph more readable;

• it will highlight the most important statement(s).

Often very short sentences may be written in list form. This style may be useful where there are a number of connecting, different, points.

HEADINGS

Where sections and subsections are used they should have meaningful and comprehensive headings. Reference to a section by paragraph numbers alone does not allow for easy reading.

Headings should not be repeated. Never subdivide a section beyond three levels, e.g. 4.1.5.8. Always ensure headings and sub-headings follow a logical sequence.

Headings should be brief and state explicitly what following text is about. General words and terms, such as 'miscellaneous' and 'other factors', should be avoided.

> *One word is good; five is acceptable; more than three-quarters of a line is probably too long.*
>
> J A Fletcher & D F Gowling
> *The Business Guide to Effective Writing*

TOPOGRAPHY

The topographical representation of a report should not be changed unless you wish to draw a matter to a reader's attention. Use of bold letters, italics and different size letters for headings should all be considered. Where headings are used, care should be taken to differentiate between major headings and sub-headings. Topography used can give a flavour to the report you can <u>underline</u>, make text **bold**, use *italics* or any combination of these styles.

GRAPHICS

Different readerships place different demands on a writer for the use of narrative, words and graphic design. Graphics, in particular, are an aid that will help your reader easily identify the type of report you are presenting. Graphics may include diagrams. It is reputed that as long ago as the 9th century Confucius stated that "a good picture is worth a thousand words". Where diagrams are used, they should be arranged carefully and account should be made of balance and contrast. Examples of different types of graphics are given below.

- **Line drawings** (black and white). These show how actions should be performed, where parts are located and provide a one dimensional view of an object.

- **Exploded drawings**. These may include CAD design of exterior and interior features, cutaways and section drawings.

- **Flow charts**. These show stages of a process or historic perspective.

- **Grey scale** (halftones). These are used in newspapers.

- **Colour** (a composite of black and yellow, red and blue). This may be used to increase impact and to focus upon specific areas.

- **Groups, columns, boxes, pie charts and histograms**.

- **Photographs**. These show an item that is existing in actuality or model form.

ORGANISING GRAPHICS

Some reports, owing to the nature of the topic, may require considerable graphic input. Technical reports, particularly those used in engineering, will require detailed graphic description of the parts used. Reports such as these should be organised using the following techniques:

- spatial;
- chronological;
- logical;
- comprehensible.

Spatial Organisation

This arrangement will set the perspective by which the reader will view an object. It may be top to bottom, front to back, left to right, right to left, etc. The sequence used will follow a determined order.

Chronological Organisation

The graphics will be arranged in chronological sequence, using the technique of spatial organisation.

Logical Organisation

A logical sequence shows how the graphics relate to each other.

Comprehensible Organisation

Graphics should not be used in isolation. They should always be titled and near to relevant text. The text should be on the same or a facing page.

REMEMBER

DO

- Be neat.
- Be conventional.
- Use short sentences.
- Use topography and graphics.
- Be chronological.
- Be logical.

DO NOT

- Make paragraphs overlong.

Chapter 6

Construction And Use Of English

This chapter will help you to:

- write clearly and effectively;
- use correct English;
- convert long sections of text into short, stylish sentences.

It will also teach you how to avoid:

- jargon;
- sexism;
- other words it is best not to use.

Construction And Use Of English

After layout and design a good report will also have the following characteristics:

- clarity;
- good use of grammar;
- accurate spelling and punctuation.

CLARITY

> *Good reports are a detailed narrative of what happened during a specific event in time. Clarity is far more important than sounding academic.*
>
> Environmental Protection Agency
> USA

The clarity of a report will depend upon the language used. A report should be written for a reader, who should be expected to understand what the report is saying. Colloquialisms and offensive language should be avoided.

Jargon and acronyms should only be used where they are in common usage and the reader would know precisely what they mean, but do not overestimate this knowledge. Reports are oftenread only by people with less technical knowledge than the writer.

WORD TO THE WISE

The clarity of a report will depend upon the language used.

GRAMMAR

Good grammatical construction ensures that a document is readable. A grammatically sound report will use good sentence and paragraph structure. Full sentences should be used and, where possible, these should be short.

Long sentences may often be divided into two or more sentences. Where a long sentence contains a number of terms it may be divided by the use of bullet points or numbering delineating each term.

The following examples compare the use of prose and bullet points.

Example 1
The Stimulation of the Training and Mobility of Researchers Programme aims to improve the quality and increase the quantity of human resources in science and technology. The programme covers research networks, research fellowships, access to large-scale facilities and accompanying measures, including euro conferences, summer schools and practical training courses.

Example 2
The Stimulation of the Training and Mobility of Researchers Programme aims to improve the quality and increase the quantity of human resources in science and technology. The programme covers:

* research networks;
* research fellowships;
* access to large-scale facilities;
* accompanying measures, including euro conferences, summer schools and practical training courses.

Many computers and word processors contain grammar checkers. One of the features that a grammar check will mention is: "This sentence is too long for grammatical construction." Sentences such as these may often be broken down by methods described above.

Active or Passive?

Use of the passive voice has become more acceptable in recent years. Where it is used, it should be used consistently. Where appropriate, use the active voice. It is clearer and shorter. For example:

Active voice   He ate fish for dinner.

Passive voice   Fish was eaten for dinner by him.

Further Examples

The footballer made a rude gesture to the crowd.
                              Active; 9 words

A rude gesture was made to the crowd by the footballer.
                              Passive; 11 words

Fred accompanied Agnes to the dance.
                              Active; 6 words

Agnes was accompanied to the dance by Fred.
                              Passive; 8 words

SPELLING AND PUNCTUATION

Although there have been many attacks on the importance of spelling, bad spelling is frowned upon. Care should be taken when using a computerised spell checker. A spell checker may not always be sensitive to meaning, unless accompanied with a grammar checker, e.g. 'their' and 'there' . On occasions, house style may dictate spellings used. Some British firms use the 'z' spelling in preference to the 's' spelling, e.g. 'organization' versus 'organisation' .

Apostrophes

Apostrophes have many uses. It is important to know when to apply them.

* Unless you are quoting an individual's response to a question, you should not contractions which include an apostrophe. Common examples of contractions are 'it's' , 'can't' and 'didn't' .

* The apostrophe is used to show possession.

Example 1

"The tiger's roar was loud."
The apostrophe in this example shows that there was one tiger that roared loudly.

Example 2

"The tigers' roar was loud."
This example show that more than one tiger was roaring loudly. (Alternatively, you could write: "The tigers were roaring loudly.")

Where a plural is irregular, e.g. children, apostrophes are placed before the letter 's', i.e. children's.

Commas and Semi-colons

Commas should be used to divide a sentence into phrases. Semi-colons are used to divide lists of nouns or phrases within a sentence. For clarity, you may wish to divide a sentence with semi-colons into one with a number of bullet points.

Brackets

Brackets should not be used in place of commas. Brackets, where used to add an anecdotal comment, could be replaced by a star [*] or superscript number [1]. The point being made could then be stated at the bottom of a page as a footnote.

Where a report's style does not allow for footnotes, brackets should only be used to indicate other relevant sections of a report, such as appendices and annexes.

Masculine and Feminine

Political correctness has caused report writers more worry than warranted. Use of words, such as, 'one', 'the person' and 'the individual', and terms such as 'he/she' tend to look untidy. By convention, the masculine use is still the norm.

Where it is felt that use of the masculine may cause offence, rephrasing using the passive voice may be possible, e.g. "The shopkeeper told the shop assistant that he should stack shelves." This could be rephrased as: "The shop assistant was told to stack shelves by the shopkeeper."

Pluralising may be another method of avoiding gender issues, e.g. "The machinist must keep her unused cotton reels for other occasions." This could be rephrased as: "Machinists must keep unused cotton reels for other occasions."

Use of the Personal Pronoun

The personal pronoun (I, me, myself) should be avoided unless the report is descriptive of actions undertaken personally, but even in these cases, it is possible to avoid the personal pronoun. Use of the personal pronoun does not negate use of the singular.

Example

"The procedures I followed were:
1. I took a saucer and cup out of a cupboard.
2. I placed the saucer on a worktop.
3. I placed the cup on the saucer.
4. I took a box of teabags out of the larder.
5. I put one teabag in the cup.
6. I poured water in the kettle.
7. I boiled the kettle.
8. I put water from the kettle into the cup.
9. I waited 90 seconds for the teabag to brew.
10. I removed the teabag with a spoon.
11. I threw the teabag into a dustbin.
12. I took milk out of the fridge.
13. I put milk into the cup.
14. I stirred the mixture.
15. I drank the tea."

Alternatively this could be written:

"Procedures followed for making tea:
1. Take a cup and saucer out of cupboard.
2. Put the saucer onto worktop.
3. Place the cup onto saucer.
4. Remove a box of teabags from the larder.
5. Placed one teabag in the cup.
6. Fill the kettle with water
7. Switch the kettle on to boil.
8. Fill the cup with boiling water.
9. Let the teabag brew for 90 seconds.
10. Remove the teabag with a spoon.
11. Place the teabag in a dustbin.
12. Take the milk from the fridge.
13. Put the milk into the cup.
14. Stir the mixture.
15. Drink the tea."

WORDS TO AVOID

All is an absolute word. It allows no exceptions. There is a tremendous difference between, "all the boys came to tea" and "all the boys in Jim's class came to tea". *Never* and *always* are also absolute words, which allow for no exceptions.

- **One.** Where possible, avoid using the term 'one' where you mean he, she, you or I.

- **He, she and they**. These words should not be used unless previously qualified, e.g. "Jill and Philip came to our house for tea. They were both looking well."

- **Words that may need clarification**. Words such as *frequently*, *often*, *regularly*, *likely* and *usually* may need to be qualified.

- **Double negatives**. Double negatives should be avoided, e.g. "It is not a bad idea that he should not avoid that person."

- **Vague expressions**. Vague expressions should be avoided, e.g. It was stated "that a good picture is better than a thousand words". Readers will want to know who made this statement.

DEFINITIONS AND THE USE OF JARGON, COLLOQUIALISMS AND ACRONYMS

Knowledge of the language and terminology used to write a report is an essential part of the communicative process between writer and reader. You must always know your readership. Never overestimate their knowledge of the subject.

Indeed, as the author of a text you may, in many cases, be regarded as the authoritative expert on the chosen subject.

Definitions

Definition distinguishes one object from another by establishing and clarifying the characteristics of an object.

Gregg Berlie
Blue Mountain Community College
Oregon

Definitions are required when:

* the audience is expanded or extended to include non-expert readers who may not understand the technical terms;
* new or rare terms are being employed, even for experts in the subject;
* terms that have multiple meanings and a specific one is required for understanding.

Gregg Berlie also describes the forms that a definition may take. These include:

* informal definitions;
* formal definitions;
* extended definitions.

Informal Definitions

These are inserted as a parenthetical addition to the text after the first reference to the term, e.g. The patient suffered from trichromatic deuteranomaly (red-green colour blindness).

Formal Definition

These are more rigid and detailed, they:

(a) include:

   (i)   the term being defined;

   (ii) the class to which it belongs;

   (iii) the attributes which distinguish it from other members of its class

(b) are inserted as a part of the text proper or as a footnote.

Footnoted definitions are a very effective way to include definitions on the page where they are needed without including them in the body text. This style allows both specialists and the layman to read the text with ease and understanding.

Extended Definition

These are included as a single or multi-paragraph entry in the text of the document or within its own heading and covering a page or more, they may also include background or origins of the term.

Types of Extended Definitions

- **Classification**: breaking a term into its types or characteristics and discussing the similarities and differences of the characteristics.

- **Comparison and contrast**: showing similarities and differences between the term being defined and another commonly understood term.

- **Description by partition**: separating a term into its parts and explaining each part individually.

- **Etymology**: showing the origin and history of a term (used with other types of definition but rarely used as the only form of definition).

- **Examples**: expanding definitions by providing synonyms, case studies and other examples for non-expert readers.

- **Negation**: explaining what the term is not or what it does not include.

- **Process**: showing how the object works in order to explain what it is.

Lastly, a definition to be avoided is a circular definition, e.g. "A food processor is an electrical kitchen appliance that processes liquid or solid food."

Jargon

The Concise Oxford Dictionary defines jargon as "unintelligible words, gibberish; barbarous or debased language; mode of speech full of unfamiliar terms".

Jargon may also include technical words and terms unintelligible to the layman but familiar to the expert. A balance needs to be sought between these two levels. When the readership of the report is specialist, technical language is acceptable, where the report is for a layperson, technical words will always need to be defined. It may also be prudent to include a glossary.

Do not refer to time frames, time spots and time intervals if they all mean the same thing; select one of these terms and tell the reader on first usage exactly what is meant by it.

Helen Lowe
Department of Computing
Napier University, Edinburgh

Colloquialisms

Colloquialisms are to be avoided. Examples of colloquialisms now in common usage include, "the full Monty", "pulling your finger out", "not my cup of tea".

Acronyms

Many subjects are laden with acronyms and abbreviations. These are used to shorten long phrases, e.g. General Certificate in School Education (GCSE). Many acronyms and abbreviations are so commonplace that they do not need explanation, USA, DNA etc.

When using an acronym for the first time, its full meaning should always be indicated after the expression, e.g. "The Qualifications and Curriculum Authority (QCA) is responsible for the assessment of National Vocational Qualifications (NVQ)".

Where acronyms are used throughout a report it may be helpful to have a glossary section.

> **WORD TO THE WISE**
>
> When using an acronym for the first time, its full meaning should always be indicated after the expression.

REMEMBER

DO

- Consider your readers.
- Check your work for grammatical and spelling errors.

DO NOT

- Use terms and words your readers are unlikely to understand.
- Use jargon.
- Use sexist language.
- Use acronyms – unless they are explained.
- Use personal pronouns.

Chapter 7

Preparation And Report Organisation

This chapter will help you to:

- be selective with your subject;
- be successful with time keeping;
- manage the organisation of report writing;
- successfully implement quality control.

Preparation And Report Organisation

PREPARATION

Being aware of your target audience and the information required is critical to the success of your report. The following procedures are helpful.

Do not take on a Subject in which you have no interest

Writing a report on a subject which has no interest to you or which you believe, from the outset, will be difficult rather than challenging is not advisable. Having no, or little knowledge on a subject, is not something to fear. Indeed, it may be helpful as you will be writing with no pre-conceived ideas or subjective thoughts. When writing a report, you should ensure that it is one in which you have no distaste for the subject and where your writing will be apt for the audience.

> *You must be comfortable with what you are preparing to do.*
>
> Ray Irving and Cathy Smith
> *No Sweat! Indispensable Guide to Reports and Dissertations*

It is equally important to be confident that you can fulfil the project on time. If the task is impossible for you to complete, say so. It is less embarrassing and time wasting for everyone if you say "no" rather than accept a project that you cannot complete, and let people down.

In a business context, failure to meet a deadline will be looked upon distastefully unless there are legitimate reasons for it.

> **WORD TO THE WISE**
>
> It is important to be confident that you can fulfil the project in time.

Confirm the Instruction

Writing a report takes time. If a report is required by a client you should confirm the instruction to proceed in writing. This will avoid any ambiguity of the terms of reference or of payment terms. In effect, it will stand as a contract in law.

Identify the Topic and the Audience

Ensure that you have understood fully the topic of the report that has been requested and also to whom the report will be circulated or made available.

Remember your Deadlines

A report is prepared for a reader or readership for a reason and this reason is often time related. A report writer will need to know when a report is required and the likely time it will take to produce it. The time needed can never be underestimated. A report should be started in good time with targets set for the finalisation of research, writing sections of the report and proof-reading.

Where material is subject to constant change (e.g. stock figures) deadline dates should be adhered. The date that information is received should also be stated.

Should a delay occur it is important to let the person or organisation commissioning the report know of this as soon as possible. Provided the reason for delay is reasonable, delays may be accepted. Failure to state delays, with the hope that they may not occur, will not be looked upon favourably should a report be submitted late or be of poor quality owing to it being rushed.

Where a delay is likely due to information changing, then the matter should be discussed with the commissioning editor.

Example 1

When I wrote a *Handbook for School Fundraising* (Kogan Page), there was an intervening general election. Noting that there were going to be immediate changes to policy and funding, a two month extension was considered prudent and advisable.

Example 2

When revising the fourth edition of *How to apply for Grants, Loans and Other Sources of Finance* (Gee Publishing Ltd), I mentioned to the editor that some European Union funding programmes were not going to be announced, in detail, until September. As a publication date was set for March, it was agreed that existing information should be provided with a rider stating that changes were likely to occur at a later date. This process would enable a limited edition of the book, for which there was considerable demand, to be published on time, allowing for a fifth edition six months later.

Determine the time needed to prepare the Report

Prepare a report diary or action plan stating daily, weekly and monthly targets or milestones to be reached. If you are using outside resources for typing, information collection or other help, estimate the time that they will take. Allow time to correct initial drafts and amended sections. Do not underestimate the time that will be needed to obtain responses to requests for information or proof-reading. Allow up to four weeks, if time is available, for this.

Items for which time will need to be allocated include the following.

- Consideration of the project – devising contents.

- General information search.

- Revision of the content list.

- Writing the introduction (many people will do this last).

- Writing of the main sections. Each section outlined in the contents list should be identified separately . At the time of writing certain information will be compiled continually, e.g. the bibliography. Keep up to date with relevant information from journals and magazines.

- Information search on specific contents.

- Choosing sources of materials, e.g. writing to sources of information.

- Collection of data, interviews, etc. (if applicable).

- Revision of the structure. Some sections will become of greater importance or lesser importance as the report writing evolves.

- Writing the summary and recommendations.

- Writing the abstract.

- Checking the contents list, introduction and abstract against the text.

- Final proof-reading, printing, binding and presentation.

- Get friends to proof-read the text. It is often easier to ask people to read smaller sections, rather than a whole report. This can be undertaken as a continuous process by one or more individuals.

When preparing a writing schedule do take account of holidays, leisure time and, of equal importance, periods when people from whom you need help are likely to be away.

Some report writers prefer to schedule their report working backwards from the date the manuscript needs to be delivered.

Undertake Research and gather Information

Only when you feel confident that the preparatory work has been completed should you begin researching the topic. Contact the people who will be providing information, visit libraries, conduct interviews etc. Ensure that you document this research as it is collected.

Organise Information

Preparing a draft or writing a contents list will prove useful for synthesizing and processing information in an orderly way. Working with a contents list will give you control over your report, keeping your writing within a defined, but flexible, framework. Contents lists should be flexible, changing as new information is received and adapting to account for the relevance, or otherwise, of information to be used.

Write the Report

When writing a report always remember the aims and objectives.

> *It is not enough to state [the objectives] at the beginning of a dissertation and then disregard them. They must remain at the forefront throughout the report.*
>
> Ray Irving and Cathy Smith
> *No Sweat! Indispensable Guide to Reports and Dissertations*

Flexibility must be allowed when writing a report. New information may arrive when a report is being written. If it arrives in time it should be considered. Most long reports are redrafted between four and twenty times before final editing takes place.

An important, but hopefully unnecessary, house rule should be to back-up your report on computer disk or with a good photocopy. Should any problem occur your loss of time will be minimised. Where an outside bureau is used for typing, it is prudent to photocopy any major text given for typing or redrafting.

WORD TO THE WISE

It is prudent to send information for checking, as soon as it is in a text-ready form, to the person whose opinion was sought.

Check Data and Statements

It is prudent to send information for checking, as soon as it is in a text-ready form, to the person whose opinion was sought. When writing to an individual or organisation for help, state the reason for your request. Ideally these should be checked with original sources. Always, and wherever possible, seek expert opinions and validate information where possible.

Mention a deadline date by which information should be received, e.g. see Appendix I. If you have had no response by the date stated, telephone the organisation to ensure that:

* the person to whom you wrote is still there;

* the letter arrived.

If the person to whom you wrote is no longer with the organisation, find out who would now be responsible for helping you.

Should a reply be given, it is both courteous and helpful for future occasions, to send a thank you letter, e.g. see Appendix II.

Edit the Report for Content and Style

Asking someone impartial to proof-read or review a report may be helpful. An outside view may highlight:

* poor writing style;

* text that cannot be readily understood;

* weaknesses in the organisation of the report;

* alternative opinions.

Ensure that the Contents List and Title match the Text

This is an essential check to ensure that in-descrepencies have not creeped in during the writing of the report and that everything is in the correct order.

Review

Review the introduction, acknowledgements and any executive summary or abstract to ensure it has evolved accurately during the report writing process.

Final Review

A final check through your report is always advisable to ensure that all the elements (covering letter, appendices, illustrations etc.) have all been included.

Submit the Report

REMEMBER

DO

- Prepare.
- Know your deadlines.
- Confirm instructions.
- Be organised.
- Make back-up copies of the draft of the report.
- Check any facts.
- Get people to help you.

DO NOT

- Ignore problems.

Chapter 8

Copyright, Ethics And Responsibility

This chapter will help you to:
- prove the quality of your research;
- know the rules of copyright;
- use quotations effectively.

It will also teach you:
- how to get help from other sources;
- to know what sensible precautions to take.

Copyright, Ethics And Responsibility

INTRODUCTION

Whilst most people would recognise that wholesale plagiarism is unacceptable, there are many situations that arise where the temptation to use other people's work, owing to its style of presentation and content, are tempting. When you use someone else's ideas or words, give credit to the source.

Courtesy, tact and honesty will usually prevail where the need to borrow other people's work would be beneficial to your own report.

Helen Lowe from the Department of Computer Studies at Napier University indicates that stating sources of information can be beneficial. Use of text would:

- furnish evidence of literature read;

- establish the body of work from which your own report arises;

- demonstrate indirectly aspects of your work which are your own and for which you should properly take credit.

NEVER COPY OTHER PEOPLE'S WORK WITHOUT PERMISSION

In academia and the commercial world, there have been many instances where text has been copied wholesale, without the permission of the original author. The financial consequences of plagiarism can be great. Where this has happened, a student will fail his paper and may possibly be disqualified for cheating. In the commercial world, the copier of text and his publisher could be sued. The copier may not only lose financially owing to damages being awarded, but may also lose out in the long term, as other publishers will be reluctant to use his services. There are, however, several instances where this commission is not so stringent.

INFORMATION IN THE PUBLIC DOMAIN

Names, addresses, telephone numbers, statistics gained from published information (but not copied in that same format) are amongst information in the public domain. Where statistical information is used, for example, gross national product of a country, distributions of wealth, it is worth referring to both the source of the information and the date it was published. The works of authors who have been dead for more than 70 years are also in the public domain.

The 50 Word Rule

Up to 50 words from an existing text may be used within the body of a report. It is always advisable to put such words in inverted commas and state their source.

The 100 Word Rule

A hundred words, being the equivalent of a quarter page of text, must not be copied without giving full reference points to the text. Whilst it is not legally necessary to seek formal permission, it is both good manners and prudent to request this.

Over 100 Words

Under no circumstances may more than hundred words of text be copied without an authors' or publishers' express permission. Where permission is granted, it should be in writing. If oral permission is given, always write to the original author or publisher to thank them for this.

PARAPHRASING

Paraphrasing may be acceptable, providing the style of the original text is changed considerably. It is prudent to refer to the source of the text within the chapter or in the bibliography section. Where appropriate you should always refer to the work of others even if you do not quote from it. It is equally important to state the judgements, insights and opinions of others, whether you quote them directly or paraphrase them.

VISUAL PRESENTATIONS

Diagrams, drawings, graphs, tables, photographs, flow charts and any manner of graphic input cannot be copied without the express permission of the original author or publisher. Always state the source and date of any statistics used.

CITATIONS

Citations or use of other people's works may be presented in a variety of ways. Where the text is less than 30 words and the text used would help a paragraph read fluently, it should be incorporated into the text. The source of the information should be given after the quotation or as a footnote.

Where larger extracts are used the text should be separated and slightly indented. There are mixed views as to whether or not quotation marks should be used in such circumstances. The author and source of the reference should always be cited.

Where a quotation of some material selectively omits words between that source's start and end points, ellipses [. . .] should be used. Where a word is changed it should be bracketed. For example, "The Lord is thy guardian . . . [He] shall guard thee from all evil. . . . [He] shall guard thy going out and thy coming in, from this time forth and for evermore." *Psalm 121.*

Where quotations contain errors, for example, a spelling mistake, by convention the term [sic] is used, in brackets, after the incorrectly used or spelt word. For example, "He wrote several leters [sic] to the general."

CHANGING INFORMATION

Where information is changed, including the style of writing, it may not be necessary to seek an original author's permission to use their text. However, this is all a matter of degree. Where text can be directly attributable to published information, permission should always be sought. Invariably, amended text will differ considerably from the original owing to its content. Under such circumstances, permission is not necessary. It is, however, recommended that sources of information are referred to either within the chapter or in a bibliography.

HOW EASY IS IT TO OBTAIN PERMISSION

Over fifteen years of professional writing I have only on one occasion been refused permission to use text. This situation occurred when the text to be used was an author's own interpretation of the law. Even in this case, it was stated in correspondence that no legal action would be taken against myself or my publishers if the text was used in the context described to them.

Asking for permission to use text has many advantages.

- It puts the report writer in a favourable position with the original author of the text. Everybody appreciates courtesy and many people are quite flattered that someone wishes to use their text.

- The text may have changed since originally written. Text taken, particularly from government departments, is often amended. It is usual for such bodies to provide new text in these circumstances.

- Asking for permission is not only good manners but also a good way to solicit new information.

Common Courtesies

When information has been supplied and permission granted, it is common courtesy to thank the person who gave it. Where substantial help is given, it is good practice to send the contributor a copy of the finished report. The practicality of this will depend on the cost.

Good manners may also be financially rewarding. For example, other publishers have so appreciated this courtesy, that they have considered me for other work. In the long term good manners can be a profitable exercise. Working ethically can only do good, not harm. Where permission to use existing text is not given initially the sharing of the problem with your academic leader, publisher, author of the work or his own publisher (depending on who is not being helpful) will often provide a remedy.

COPYING FROM THE INTERNET

Copying text from the internet does fall under copyright law, even though the information is in the public domain. The information obtained from the internet also has other dangers associated with it. It is sometime inaccurate. It is good practice to check the information obtained from the internet both with the originator of the information and through other sources.

Again, I can give an anecdotal story on the inaccuracy of information obtained from the internet. When writing my book *A Handbook of School Fundraising* (Kogan Page) I came across a report on moral and spiritual education for children. Being the first report I had read on that subject, it appeared to be well researched, particularly as it had an extensive bibliography. The only problem with the report is that it was inaccurate. The author had mixed up legislation and misinterpreted the law. Fortunately, these errors were pointed out to me by several other organisations with whom I had close contact and from whom I sought advice and guidance as proof-readers.

Indemnities

No matter how cautious you are, a report may contain information that is inaccurate. A missing word may completely change the meaning of an intended text. For example, "Thou shall not steal" and "Thou shall steal".

An indemnity will normally state that "no responsibility for loss occasioned to any person acting or refraining from action as a result of any material in this publication can be accepted by the author or publisher".

Responsibility

An author is responsible for his work. Whilst indemnities are prudent, they will not protect the report writer from negligence or recklessness. A report writer has a duty of care to his readership.

Defamation

A report, even where its contents are accurate, that condones or condemns the actions of an individual or an organisation, may be defamatory. A written defamation is known as libel. Where the libel is untrue, and can be proven to have damaged a person's or an organisation's reputation, income or well-being, the

WORD TO THE WISE

A report, even where its contents are accurate, that condones or condemns the actions of an individual or an organisation, may be defamatory.

offended party may sue the report writer and his
publishers for libel. Many well-known cases have
occurred, over the years, particularly against newspapers in the United Kingdom.

REMEMBER

DO

- Make sure that you know when permission to use information is obligatory.
- Ask for permission to use existing text.
- Remember that paraphrasing may be plagarism.
- Learn how to use quotations.
- Indemnify your work.

DO NOT

- Copy other peoples' work without permission.
- Rely on one source of information.
- Slander.

Chapter 9

Using Reports For Presentations

This chapter will tell you how to:

- present your report orally;
- feel at ease when giving a presentation;
- present yourself;
- answer difficult questions from an audience.

Useful Reports For Presentations

An objective of report writing is "to clearly and coherently express and present what you have come to know, for yourself and for others". (Blue Mountain Community College.)

Written reports are often used as the basis for discussion. Oral presentations will examine an author's understanding of their work and question elements that are polemical. The points given below will refer to the oral presentation of a report at a meeting or seminar.

KNOW WHAT YOU HAVE WRITTEN

It is worth emphasising the above heading, even though it would seem to be unnecessary. It is far too easy to forget the context in which certain statements were made, no matter how intimate you are with your work.

When attending a presentation it is helpful to have available:

- a copy of the report;
- a separate copy of contents list with annotations of the content of each section;
- supporting documents and visual aids.

KNOW YOUR AUDIENCE

An oral presentation will always be made to an interested individual or group of people. Fortunately, few people are likely to ask questions to 'catch you out'. Try to find out, in advance, the composition of your audience and how many people you will be speaking to.

WORD TO THE WISE

Try to find out, in advance, the composition of your audience and how many people you will be speaking to.

Knowledge of the audience may help you with your presentation as the greater the audience, the greater will be the formality needed. For example, an expert in a certain discipline may try to link his knowledge to a question. If a report is well prepared, and checked through by others before the final draft is written, there are unlikely to be awkward questions that cannot be answered effectively. Questions will be of two types:

- inquisitive questions;
- elaborative questions.

Inquisitive Questions

Inquisitive questions will ask how evidence was accumulated, what methodology you used in writing the report and other questions of fact.

Elaborative Questions

Elaborative questions will seek further information on a particular point. The question may request greater detail on one or other aspect of the report or question the emphasis placed upon it.

Whether a question is inquisitive or elaborative do not guess answers. It is far better to say that your research did not cover a certain point or that you do not know an answer. Giving incorrect information will weaken all arguments as well as the quality of your report.

KNOW THE PURPOSE OF THE PRESENTATION

Presentations of reports may be for several purposes.

- **To persuade or inspire**, e.g. to persuade an organisation to buy a product or service.

- **To inform**, e.g. to demonstrate to an audience that you have sufficiently and adequately researched a subject and been able to draw information together.

- **To instruct or tell**, e.g. the use of a report as a basis for providing information.

- **To command**, e.g. to state a course of action to be taken, based upon information given.

- **To summarise**, e.g. to give a brief overview of what your report is about.

Do not assume that your audience is interested in your report. You have to make them interested. Know how long you will be required to speak.

COLLABORATIVE PRESENTATIONS

Reports written collaboratively may need to be presented by the authors. In such situations it is important that you have an overview of the report and detailed knowledge of your own particular section and know how it links in with your colleagues' work. It is acceptable to refer a questioner to the appropriate expert in your team. It is unacceptable:

- to contradict one of your team;
- to argue against the information stated in the report. The time for disagreement is when it is being written, not at the time of presentation;
- to denigrate a member of your team.

REHEARSE

Time and plan your presentation. It is helpful to rehearse your presentation in front of a friend or colleague who has some knowledge of the subject area. Both the content of the presentation and answers to likely questions should be rehearsed. Ask them for feedback on content, style and delivery. Be happy with friendly and constructive criticism. This will help you to iron out weaknesses in the presentation. Unless stated otherwise, leave about 20 per cent of the time at the end of the presentation for questions. Where audio-visual aids are used, include a rehearsal using them.

> **WORD TO THE WISE**
>
> It is helpful to rehearse your presentation in front of a friend or colleague who has some knowledge of the subject area.

KNOW YOUR SURROUNDINGS

Arrive at the place of presentation early. Test any audio-visual equipment to be used. Familiarise yourself with the room and place all equipment (including stands, chairs, etc.) where you want them to be. Find out who will be introducing you and enquire how they will be doing this and what they will say.

USE OF VISUAL AIDS

Visual aids are good prompters for making a presentation. They also help break up a presentation making it more interesting to an audience. The value of visual aids will depend upon the nature of the presentation.

Supporting documents may be useful 'memory joggers'. Visual aids (e.g. slides, models, etc.) should be collated in the order of presentation. This will allow you to present your report in an orderly, relaxed and efficient manner, giving an air of spontaneity. Searching for documents during a presentation is clumsy and indicates that you are not well prepared. Practice using the supporting information. Be selective when using visual aids. Too many may prove distracting rather than helpful.

BASIC PRESENTATION SKILLS

Voice Quality Control your speed of delivery. Speak at a slow, firm, deliberate pace. Take particular care if your report is critical of someone or something. Always try to control emotions.

Language Avoid swearing, sexist or racist jokes, slang, name dropping, personal attacks or abuse, guessing answers, emphasising your own importance. Avoid using 'I' or 'me' too often. Only use humour if you are confident that it will work. Punch lines must be rehearsed. Humour should only be used to support the text not in its own right.

Body Language   Body language is vital. Greg Berlie, of Blue Mountain Community College states that the impact of any communication is: "7 per cent verbal; 38 per cent tonal; 55 per cent visual."

Body language techniques include "lifting your spine, dropping your shoulders, keeping the front of your body long and keeping the back of the neck long". *Positive Management Assertiveness for Managers*, Paddy O'Brien.

The presentation may be formal or informal. Wear good, conservative clothes. These should include a pair of comfortable shoes. If in doubt, wear a suit.

If standing, do not place your feet too close or too far apart. Keep your hands loose in front of you. Avoid fidgeting or swinging from side to side. Natural hand movements are an asset rather than a liability. Avoid irritating mannerisms, e.g. stroking hair away from your face. Above all, smile.

It is noticeable that the majority of an audience will remember what is said at the beginning of a presentation and at the end. These two parts of any oral presentation must be thoroughly rehearsed.

Eye Contact   Do not focus on one person. Try to shift your gaze across the room or across your audience.

CONTROL

Where possible, control the presentation. Do not read your report. Use of palm or memory cards, one-word notes, will enable you to remember the salient points and present them in a natural manner. Request that all questions are kept to the end of your presentation.

QUESTIONS AND ANSWERS

It is helpful to repeat questions asked. If they are long questions, summarise them. Doing this will allow you to play for time, thereby collecting your thoughts ready for a reply. It also helps with a presentation as some of the audience may not have heard the question.

Do not give open ended answers. This would result in a debate between you and one member of the audience. If you do not know the answer to a question do not guess it. Never be afraid to say that you do not have knowledge on a particular point. If you do not have knowledge, it is likely to be for a valid reason. This, for example, could be stated, "The point raised was outside the scope of this report."

WORD TO THE WISE

Do not give open ended answers. This would result in a debate between you and one member of the audience.

REMEMBER

DO

- Know your subject.
- Know your audience.
- Rehearse.
- Dress appropriately.
- Arrive early.
- Bring memory joggers.
- Think before speaking.
- Speak slowly.
- Smile.

DO NOT

- Contradict a colleague.
- Guess.
- Be afraid to say, "I do not know."

Appendix 1

Sample Letter Requesting Help With The Checking Of Information

Ann Henderson
Pre-School Learning Alliance
69 King's Cross Road
LONDON
WC1X 9LL

1 November 1998

Dear Mrs Henderson

Re: A Handbook of School Fundraising

I am writing the above book for Kogan Page. One section of the book outlines assistance and financial support that is available for children under the age of five years.

I would be grateful if you would look at the enclosed text, in which your organisation is mentioned, to ensure it is accurate.

I would appreciate your reply by 30 November to ensure that publication deadlines set are reached.

Thanking you in advance for your help.

Yours sincerely

Harris Rosenberg
Enc

Appendix 2

Sample Letter Thanking A Contributor For Support

Ann Henderson
Pre-School Learning Alliance
69 King's Cross Road
LONDON
WC1X 9LL

2 December 1998

Dear Mrs Henderson

Re: A Handbook of School Fundraising

Thank you for your letter dated 25 November. I am grateful for the comments you made and for the further information you have supplied. I have amended the text to account for these.

Yours sincerely

Harris Rosenberg
Enc

Note: It is not always necessary to send a copy of a report to those who help you. However, where substantial help is given, it is polite to do so.

Bibliography

BOOKS

Concise Oxford Dictionary of Current English, 5th edition (Oxford University Press, Oxford) 1964.

Longman Dictionary of the English Language, 2nd edition (Longman Group UK Ltd, London) 1991.

Fletcher, JA andGowring, DF: *The Business Guide to Effective Writing* (Kogan Page, London) 1987.

Irving, R and Smith, C: *No Sweat! The Indispensable Guide to Reports and Dissertations* (Institute of Management Foundation) 1998.

Lewis, R and Inglis, J *Report Writing* (National Extension College, Cambridge) 1982.

Singer, Revd S: *Authorised Daily Prayer Book of the United Hebrew Congregations of the British Commonwealth of Nations* 1979.

Stewart, I: *The Business Writing Workbook: a guide to defensive writing skills* (Kogan Page, London) 1987.

JOURNALS

Professional Manager (Volume 7, Number 1) January 1998.

INTERNET SITES

AltaVista: Simple Query: (01/03/98)
http://www.dcs.napier.ac.uk/~helen

Delivery Checklist: (27/11/97)
*http://www.1.fste.ac.cowan.edu.au/AAECP/oral_pre.4/
delivery/delivery.htm*

Freshman English Composition (Distant learning) (15/
03/98)
http://staff.bmcc.cc.or.us/~gberlie/wr/122/wr/22.htm

Freshman English Composition (Distant learning
Spring Term 1997) (15/03/98)
http://staff.bmcc.cc.or.us/~cleguin/

General Report Writing: (26/11/97)
*http://www.1.fste.ac.cowan.edu.au/AAECP/writ_ski/
rept_gen/rept_gen-htm*

Getting Started with Interactive Programming (22/12/
97)
*http:/www.sas.com/usergroups/sugi/sugi19/
abs94.html*

Guidance on the Production of BSC and MSC
Dissertations (26/11/97)
*http://www.dcs.napier.ac.uk/~helen/teaching/projects/
report97.htm*

Inspection: The Report (17/02/98)
*http://www.epa.gov/r10earth/offices/oea/ieu/
manual/inspct04.htm*

Interactive Report Writing with the Report Procedure
(26/11/97)   .
*http://www.sas.com/usergroups/sugi/sugi19/
abs96.html*

Introduction to using the SAS System Interactively for Batch Users (22/12/97)
http://www.sas.com/usergroups/sugi/sugi19/abs9e.html

Long Report: (27/11/97)
http://www1.fste.ac.cowan.edu.au/AAECP/tec_rep/long_rep/longreps.htm

Making that Presentation (20/12/97)
http://www.businessconnections.bt.com/guides/c36/

Meetings (19/04/98)
http://www.smartbiz.com/sbs/arts/afm1.htm

Mission Statement (26/11/97)
http://www.cedarville.edu/employee/harners/mission.htm

The Money Game: Preparing the Budget and Financial Reporting (19/04/98)
http://www.emich.edu/public/ord/handbook/budget.html

Packaging and Presentation of Reports and Other Material: (27/11/97)
http://www.1.fste.ac.cowan.edu.au/AAECP/writ_ski/package/package.htm

Report Contents: "The 5 "Ws" (26/11/97)
http://www.epa.gov/r10earth/offices/oea/ieu/manual/inspct06.htm

Report Writing Skills (26/11/97)
http://www.chl.co.uk/c600.htm

Report Writing: Words and Phrases to avoid (26/11/97)
http://www.epa.gov/r10earth/offices/oea/ieu/manual/inspct07.htm

Short Reports: (27/11/97)
http://www.1.fste.ac.cowan.edu.au/AAECP/tec_rep/
shrt_rep/shrt_rep.htm

Syllabus for Technical Report Writing (26/11/97)
http://www.staff.bmcc.cc.or.us~gberlie/wr227/
wr227syl.htm

Technical Report Writing (Distant Learning) (15/03/98)
http://staff.bmcc.cc.or.us/~wr227/wr227.htm

Using Audiovisual Equipment Effectively: (27/11/97)
http://www.1.fste.ac.cowan.edu.au/AAECP/oral_pre.4/
audiovis/audiovis.htm

Write the Report as you did the Inspection (17/02/98)
http://www.epa.gov/r10earth/offices/oea/ieu/
manual/inspect05.htm

Writing the Report (17/02/98)
http://www.epa.gov/r10earth/offices/oea/ieu/
manual/inspct05.htm